SOPHIA HUDSON

MANGA COOKBOOK

Delicious Recipes Inspired by Your
Favorite Manga Characters
(2024 Recipes for Beginners)

Copyright © 2024 by Sophia Hudson

All rights reserved. No part of this publication may be reproduced, stored or transmitted in any form or by any means, electronic, mechanical, photocopying, recording, scanning, or otherwise without written permission from the publisher. It is illegal to copy this book, post it to a website, or distribute it by any other means without permission.

First edition

This book was professionally typeset on Reedsy. Find out more at reedsy.com

Contents

1 Introduction   1
2 Chapter 1 – Food Wars   3
3 from Different Anime Series   20
4 Chapter 3 – Japanese Sweet Stuff   44
5 Conclusion   55

1

Introduction

Manga has a strong influence on practically every aspect of Japanese culture, including music, sports, shooting pools, and cuisine. Similar to movies in the United States, it serves as a storytelling medium in Japan. When Food Manga first debuted in the 1980s, Japan's economy was booming. The basis for this anime series was the first Oishinbo, which ran for nearly 20 years. Comics about food, such Solitary Gourmet, Food Wars, and others, revolve around cooking and conflict.

Nobunaga worked as a young cook at a conventional, upscale hotel on the front lines of battle in the fifteenth century. He gets hired as a dishonest warlord's chef and uses his culinary prowess to boost the spirits of his soldiers. He can entice enemy warriors off the battlefield with his potent cooking abilities.

The background is a love story taking place in the manga kitchen. The protagonist of the tale, innocuously enough, wishes to learn how to make pancakes or something else. As the plot develops, it becomes more romantic, criminal, mysterious, and intriguing. The cuisines always take center stage at these occasions.

Toriko is a hunter of uncommon substances in this narrative. Toriko possesses superhuman powers to acquire uncommon substances and get past any impediment. Manga Cookbook provides step-by-step instructions for 25 different dishes. Yakitate is exceptionally skilled in the kitchen when it comes to creating bread. These comic series center on Makito Koenji, a curry cook. Even in the face of unfavorable circumstances, he can keep the restaurant operating. For lovers of Italy, The Bambino is a spot where.

Manga books are mostly meant to provide detailed recipes for Japanese foods. You may make delectable Japanese food by following these tasty recipes:

2

Chapter 1 – Food Wars

Shokugeki No Souma Treats

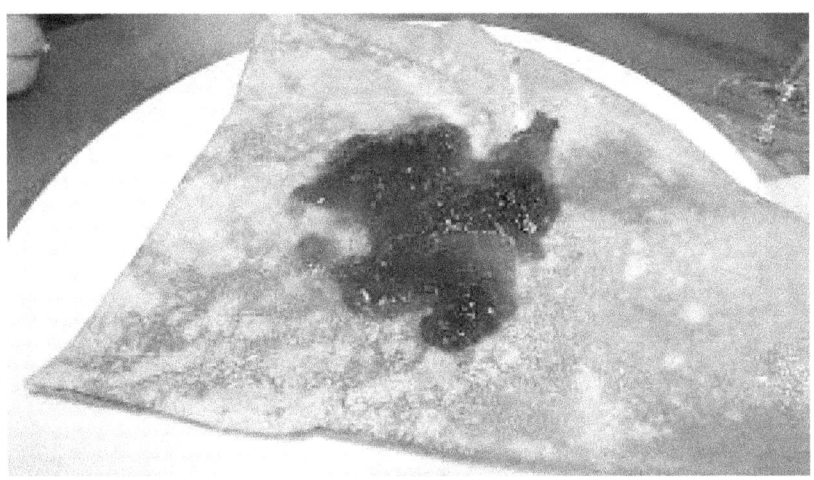

The story of young Soma Yukihira, who aspires to become a chef in his father's competing restaurant, is told by Shokugeki-no Souma. His goal was to outdo his father's culinary prowess. When Soma graduates, his father, Joichiro Yukihira, takes a new job that requires him to close the store and tour the entire world. However, Joichiro challenges Soma to successfully complete his training in a cooking school, where only 10% of students were able to graduate, which reignites his fighting spirit. He makes new friends and participates in odd activities to advance his culinary abilities and objectives.

    This book, written by great culinary students, tells the story of a conflict in the culinary arts.

Curry Rice with Pineapple by Miyoko Houjou

Cooking Time: 1 hour
Servings: 6
Ingredients:

- One ripe sweet pineapple;
- four green onions (quarter-inch chunks);
- three cloves of chopped garlic
- One tablespoon of oil;
- two lightly beaten eggs;
- two cups of long-grain rice, either brown or white
- One cup of diced carrots and peas;

- ½ teaspoon of salt;
- ¼ teaspoon of black pepper
- ¼ teaspoon of powdered turmeric
- ¼ teaspoon of coriander spice and ¼ teaspoon of chili flakes
- ¼ cup of roasted cashews without salt and 1 tablespoon of coconut milk
- One tablespoon of soy sauce
- One pound of boneless boiled pork or chicken flesh (cut into cubes)

Directions:

Get the oven approximately to 375F.

Slice your pineapple in half, then remove the entire flesh, being careful to preserve the skin. Dice the pineapple flesh and set aside nearly a cup.

Using a paper towel, pat both pineapple shells dry. Cover the pineapple leaves with aluminum foil. It will stop the leaves from burning. To dry them out, bake your pineapple boats for nearly five minutes.

In a wok or skillet, heat one tablespoon of cooking oil over high heat. Stir-fry the onion and garlic for a minute after adding them.

Only half of the beaten eggs should be added to the wok; simmer without stirring for nearly 30 seconds. To the wok, add the cooked rice, pork, carrots, peas, and the remaining eggs. Add chili flake, pepper, salt, and coriander.

Kolivartha Curry by Akira Hayama

Cooking Time: 30 minutes
Servings: 4
Ingredients:

- 1 1/2 pounds of skin-on chicken thigh fillets;
- 4 cloves of minced garlic
- One inch of minced ginger, one diced onion, one diced and deseeded tomato, and two tablespoons of oil
- Half a cup of ground almonds;
- one teaspoon of garam masala;
- one tablespoon of ground coriander;
- one teaspoon of ground cumin;
- half to one teaspoon of chili powder
- One half cup of coconut milk;
- two to three whole cloves;

- half a teaspoon of turmeric; and
- Chopped cilantro for serving;
- Salt to taste;
- Fresh lemon juice from one to two lemons

Directions:

After rinsing each chicken piece, blot dry with a paper towel. Set it away. Place garlic, onion, and ginger in a food processor or blender. Add tomatoes to this mixture after pulsing these components for a few minutes to create a smooth paste. After pulsing for a few more minutes, put it away.

Place a pan over a medium heat source. Oil should be heated before adding the chicken, which should be sautéed for a few minutes to lightly brown all sides. After removing the chicken from the pan, set it aside.

Cook the tomato mixture in this skillet for around five to six minutes. Add the nuts and ground spices to this mixture while stirring regularly. Well-stir this mixture. Bring back the frying.

Char Okakiage by Souma Yukihira

Cooking Time: 15 to 30 minutes
Servings: 2
Ingredients:

- Twelve ounces of ki (remove the peanuts from the ki)
- Four or six fish fillets
- One cup of flour
- One whisked egg

Directions:

Oil should be heated in a deep saucepan. Break up the kaki into small pieces and set it aside. After patting each fillet dry with a paper towel, place it in the flour basin. Give them a good toss to evenly coat each fillet in flour.

Coat each fish fillet with beaten egg. Move them right away

to the bowl of kaki crumbs that has been crushed. Throw them with skill. Fry them in an oil-filled deep saucepan until they turn golden brown. Additionally, fillets can be prepared in an air fryer. Accompany with your preferred sauce and mayonnaise.

Roast Pork by Souma Yukihira

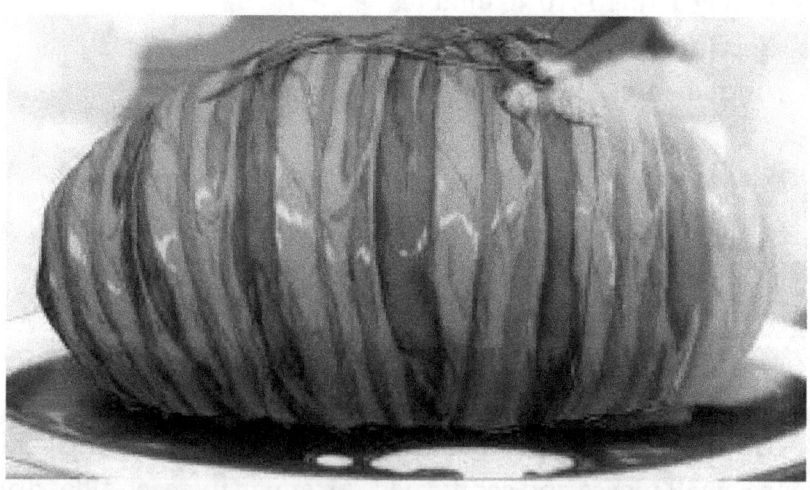

Cooking Time: 10 to 20 minutes
  Servings: 4 to 6
  Ingredients:

- Two Eringi mushrooms, seven potatoes,
- eleven medium-sized thick bacon slices,
- one chopped onion, a few sprigs of rosemary,
- four tablespoons of red wine,
- and one teaspoon of sweet sake
- One teaspoon of soy sauce,
- one tablespoon of butter,
- and a handful of watercress leaves

Directions:

Cut each potato in half from the middle and steam to soften it.

In a food processor, finely chop the onion and Eringi mushrooms, then set them aside. Steamed potatoes should be mashed and placed in a bowl. To form a medium-sized log, combine the minced onion and Eringi mushrooms in the potato bowl. Wrap the bacon slices around the potato log one at a time, and tie cooking twine around the sprigs of rosemary. Holding the pork log together is crucial.

To produce crispy bacon, roast it in a wire rack or baking sheet that has been greased, then bake it at 200 degrees for about 35 minutes.

Sauce:

To make the sauce, combine red wine, sweet sake, and soy sauce in a bowl.

Transfer them to a saucepan and bring to a boil. Cook for one minute after adding one tablespoon of butter. Drizzle the bacon log with this sauce, then top with watercress leaves. Warm up the food.

Chaliapin Steak by Souma Yukihira

Cooking Time: 1 hour
  Servings: 2
  Ingredients:
   • One chopped red onion; two boneless steaks; one tablespoon soy sauce; one-and-a-half teaspoon Sriracha
   • Honey: 1 tsp
   • 1/4 tsp balsamic vinegar
   • Two teaspoons of unsalted butter

• Finely chopped chives as a garnish

Directions:

Score steaks using a single grid pattern in the first phase. Use a meat tenderizer or the back of a hefty knife to tenderize meat. Meat needs to be given some solid blows.

Now take a plate and fill the bottom with some onion. Arrange onions on a plate, then place the steak on top of the onions. Cover this dish with clingfilm and refrigerate for approximately 30 to 45 minutes.

After removing the onions from the meat, season with salt and pepper. Cook the meat for a few minutes on each side after greasing a nonstick pan. Continue flipping the sides since you must cook from both sides. Steaks should be taken out of the pan and set aside. Use a comparable pan without cleaning it.

Monkfish Dobujiru by Megumi Tadokoro

Cooking Time: 30 minutes
Servings: 2
Ingredients:

- 500g of monkfish fillet;
- 80g of monkfish liver;
- ¼ head of bok choy;
- 1/6 Japanese pumpkin
- Daikon radish: 1/6;
- burdock root: 1.
- One pack of enoki mushrooms

- One kelp and bonito soup stock liter;
- one grilled tofu block;
- one white onion;
- one tablespoon of oil
- Two tablespoons of curry powder
- Four teaspoons of Awase Miso and four tablespoons of Soy Sauce
- Sake (100 cubic centimeters);
- Mirin (two teaspoons);
- Grated ginger (one teaspoon).

Finishing Touches:
- Two cups of cooked rice.
- One beaten egg; one chopped spring onion

Directions:

To start, blanch the monkfish fillet by submerging it in hot water for around 20 seconds, or until it turns white. Now, give it a brief dip in the icy water and set it aside.

Chop the bok choy and tofu into tiny pieces. Set them aside. Cut the pumpkin and burdock root into thin pieces. Set them aside. Cut the daikon radish into quarters and then cut these quarters. Scallion should be cut diagonally and set aside.

Split the mushroom bases carefully, then split each one in half. Cut the liver of your monkfish flat using a knife. Set aside each of these components.

Warm up some oil in a pan. Simmer the monkfish liver for a few minutes after adding the curry powder. As soon as you smell curry powder strongly, you can.

Karaage Roll by Ikumi Mito and Souma Yukihira

Cooking Time: 1 hour 20 minutes
 Servings: 2
 Ingredients:

- 450 grams of boneless,
- 2.5-centimeter chicken thighs
- One tablespoon of grated ginger and one clove of grated garlic
- Two tablespoons of soy sauce,
- one tablespoon of sake,
- two teaspoons of granulated sugar,
- one-third cup of potato starch,

- vegetable oil for frying,
- and a lemon for garnish

Directions:
Place the soy sauce, sugar, sake, ginger, and garlic in a bowl.

Mix these components thoroughly. Coat each chicken piece evenly by adding them all to the soy sauce mixture. Place this bowl in the refrigerator for nearly an hour with a lid on. One inch of oil should be added to a pot with a sturdy bottom, and it should be heated for a few minutes to reach 360 degrees Fahrenheit. Using tongs, line a single wire rack with two paper towels. Transfer potato starch to a basin.

To ensure that every piece of chicken is evenly coated, add a few pieces to the bowl of potato starch and mix thoroughly. Coat each piece gradually in starch and cook in small batches over low heat in heated oil.

Rainbow Terrine by Souma Yukihira and Megumi

Tadokoro

Cooking Time: 4 minutes
Servings: 2
Ingredients:

- Leaves of Swiss chard: 5 to 6
- Garlic, minced: two cloves
- Bell peppers: 1 (red), 1" broad slice
- Three carrots, thinly sliced lengthwise

- Summer squash (yellow and crookneck): two 5-inch lengthwise thin slices
- 5" zucchini pieces: 2
- One sliced eggplant; one cup of low-fat ricotta cheese
- Two tablespoons of chopped thyme and rosemary might be added.

Directions:

Place the eggplant, yellow squash, and zucchini in a colander. Apply a layer of salt to the veggies and set aside (while preparing the remaining dish) to allow the salt to draw out the water.

Set oven temperature to almost 425. Place the chard in a pot of boiling water and cook for two to three minutes. Remove the chard and submerge it for a short while in cold water. Arrange the red peppers on a baking sheet and season them with salt and oil. To make the skin brown, bake them for almost ten minutes.

In the interim, line a loaf pan or plastic container with a piece of plastic wrap. After drying each chard leaf, arrange it in a pan so that.

3

from Different Anime Series

Several recipes from various anime shows are included in this chapter. These are incredibly tasty and simple to make at home recipes:

Vegetable Rice from Cooking Papa

FROM DIFFERENT ANIME SERIES

Cooking Time: 20 minutes
Servings: 2 to 4
Ingredients:

- One tablespoon of sesame oil
- Cooked long-grain rice: 4 cups
- One tablespoon of mirin and two teaspoons of soy sauce
- One cup of thawed frozen edamame beans

- ¼ cup pickled ginger;
- Purple basil leaves for serving;
- Shredded nori for serving;
- Black sesame seeds for garnish

Directions:

Take a pan and heat sesame oil in this pan over high flame. Cook the rice in this pan for about two minutes after adding it. Add the mirin and soy sauce, and simmer for another three minutes or so. Spoon this mixture into dishes and garnish with edamame, pickled ginger, and basil. To serve, top with nori, togarashi, and sesame seeds.

Note: Four cups of cooked rice are equal to one and a third cups of uncooked rice.

FROM DIFFERENT ANIME SERIES

Omu-rice

Cooking Time: 25 minutes
  Servings: 2 to 3
  Ingredients:
  • Medium onion: ½

- One chicken thigh, rinsed and patted dry with paper towel;
- One tablespoon of olive oil
- ½ cup mixed vegetables;
- Salt to taste
- Ground black pepper: according to taste
- Cooked Japanese rice: 1½ cups
- One tablespoon of ketchup; one teaspoon of soy sauce

One Omelet
- Large egg: 1
- Milk: 1 tablespoon
- Olive oil: 1 tablespoon
- Cheddar cheese: 3 tablespoons

Directions:

Dice the chicken and onion into 1 cm or ½ inch chunks. Set them aside.

Take a pan and heat it by adding oil to it. Saute chopped onions for one to two minutes, or until they become tender. Cook the chicken for a few minutes, or until the pink hue vanishes.

Add the veggies and season with salt and pepper. It's time to thoroughly stir in the rice. Toss the rice with the ketchup and soy sauce, mixing everything thoroughly. Wash your cooking pan after transferring the rice and chicken combination to one area. Set aside the platter of rice. In a bowl, whisk together the egg and milk. Reapply oil to your pan and set the heat to medium. When the pan is heated.

FROM DIFFERENT ANIME SERIES

Tonkatsu

.

Cooking Time: 10 to 15 minutes
Servings: 2
Ingredients:

- One pound of boneless pork chops
- And one-fourth cup of flour
- One whipped egg
- One to two cups of breadcrumbs or panko
- Salt and pepper to taste;
- Oil to suit needs

Directions:

To acquire the correct thickness, cut and pound the pork slices. Sort flour, breadcrumbs, and whisked egg into three different bowls. To suit your tastes, you can add salt and pepper to the flour.

Each pork cutlet should be thoroughly floured before being dipped into the dish of whisked egg. Lastly, push the breadcrumbs into the bowl to coat all of the pork chunks.It's time to fry the pork by heating oil in a pan over medium heat. Coat and fry pig chunks till golden brown on all sides. Pork can also be fried in a deep fryer. Place the cooked pork onto a paper towel-lined platter.Accompany with miso soup, rice, and sliced cabbage.

Chicken Katsu

Cooking Time: 20 minutes
  Servings: 6

- **Ingredients:**
  - Six skinless, boneless breasts (each about 1/2 inch thick)
  - Beaten egg: 1 1/2 cups breadcrumbs;
  - salt and pepper to taste; 1 cup frying oil
  - Three tablespoons of all-purpose flour

Directions:

The chicken breast must first be seasoned with salt and pepper on both sides. Divide the flour, beaten egg, and breadcrumbs among shallow bowls. Dust your chicken pieces with flour, then shake off any extra. To cover all sides, dip chicken pieces into whisked eggs and then press into bread crumbs.

It's time to preheat a frying skillet with 1/4 inch of oil over medium heat. Add coated chicken to the heated oil. Cook until golden, about 3 to 4 minutes on each side. Serve over white rice or with sauce.

Chicken Nabe

Cooking Time: 45 minutes
Servings: 4
Ingredients:

- One tablespoon of olive oil
- Four cups of chicken stock; 700g of fillets of chicken breast
- Two carrots, chopped lengthwise
- Chopped Chinese Cabbage (Wombok): ½
- ¼ cup miso paste
- Sake for cooking: two tablespoons
- Two teaspoons of soy sauce and one tablespoon of caster sugar
- 2 trimmed shallots;
- To serve, steam rice

Directions:

Heat oil in a deep pan over a medium heat source. Cook the chicken pieces thoroughly on both sides for about seven minutes. Move the chicken pieces to a single platter and shred them. Set this platter aside. Simmer the carrots and chicken stock in the same pan for five minutes. Cook the cabbage for four minutes after adding it to the pan.

In a bowl, mix together sake, soy sauce, sugar, and miso. Pour in portion of the cooking pan's liquid and thoroughly combine. Transfer this blend into the frying pan and gently stir to fully dissolve the miso.

Spoon soup into serving bowls and garnish with green onions and shredded chicken. Accompany with steaming rice.

Rice Balls (Onigiri)

Cooking Time: 30 minutes
Servings: 8
Ingredients:

- One pound of cooked ground chicken,
- eight umeboshi (dried plums),
- one pound of short-grain rice,
- eight nori, and salt to taste

Directions:

Cooking the rice to your own liking is the first step. Make sure they're warm enough for you to handle with ease. Cut each nori sheet into nine strips.

Place the rice and ground chicken in a bowl. Stir them thoroughly.

To prevent salt from clinging to your hands, wet both of your hands and sprinkle them with salt. Create an indentation in the center of one handful of the cooked rice and chicken mixture by shaping it into a triangle. Place one umeboshi piece into the indentation.

Serve the rice and umeboshi with your preferred sauce after wrapping them in strips of nori.

Salted Salmon

Cooking Time: 3 days or more
Servings: 4
Ingredients:

- One pound of scaled salmon pieces
- one tablespoon of sake
- 1 to 1 ½ tablespoons of sea salt

Directions:

Place the salmon chunks in a single layer on a platter. After adding sake to the fish, let it sit for five minutes.

Every piece of salmon should be salted, and the top should have a little more salt applied. Line a paper plate with these pieces, then cover with a paper towel. All of the fish pieces can be stacked into two layers by dividing them with paper towels. Fish pieces should be covered and refrigerated for nearly three days.

After three days, rinse the salmon pieces to get rid of any excess salt, then fry them in a single layer on a parchment paper-lined tray. Cook everything thoroughly by broiling (let the skin brown). It might take five or six minutes. Make sushi or serve with rice.

Tempura Sauce

Cooking Time: 20 minutes
Servings: 1 cup
Ingredients:

- ¾ cup of dashi stock
- Three tablespoons of Japanese soy sauce,
- two tablespoons of mirin,
- and two teaspoons of sugar
- Peeled daikon: 2 inches

Directions:

Add the sugar, dashi, mirin, and soy sauce to a pot. For the sugar to dissolve, let it simmer over low heat. After turning off the heat, set it aside to cool.

Before serving, grate the daikon using the small holes of a cheese grater and stir in the sauce. Before combining, take sure to squeeze off the water from the grated daikon. As a dipping sauce, serve.

Tempura

Cooking Time: 35 minutes
Servings: 6
Ingredients:

- One cup of all-purpose flour,
- two teaspoons of cornstarch,
- one pinch of salt,
- and one cup of water
- One egg yolk;
- two lightly whisked egg whites;
- one pound of medium shrimp (skin and vein removed);

- two cups of vegetable oil for frying

Directions:

Heat the oil in a deep fryer to almost 375 degrees Fahrenheit. In a bowl, stir together flour, cornstarch, and salt. Create a hole in the center of the mixture of flour. Pour water and egg yolk into this hole. Mix them to create a moist, lumpy batter. Add the beaten egg whites and whisk.

To coat every shrimp, dip each one in the batter one at a time. Batter shouldn't be applied to the tails. Deep fry a few of breaded shrimp. They should be fried for about a minute to turn golden brown. Repeat these steps with every shrimp. Empty onto a paper towel-lined plate. Accompany with your preferred sauce!

Gyu-don

Cooking Time: 40 minutes
Servings: 4
Ingredients:

- Steamed Japanese rice: four cups
- One pound of thinly sliced beef loin and one sliced onion
- 1 1/3 cups of dashi soup

- Five tablespoons of soy sauce
- Three tablespoons of mirin,
- two tablespoons of sugar,
- and one tablespoon of sake
- Pickled ginger, or benezoga, is an optional garnish.

Directions:

Place the sake, sugar, dashi, mirin, and soy sauce in a skillet and bring to a simmer over medium heat. To soften the onions, add the onion slices to the soy sauce mixture and boil for a few minutes. When the meat is cooked, add it to the frying pan and simmer it for ten to fifteen minutes.

Place the steamed rice in a deep bowl, add the beef and benishoga on top, and then cover the rice with liquid. Warm up the food.

Bento Tamago-yaki

Cooking Time: 25 minutes
  Servings: 6
  Ingredients:
  • Eggs: 4
  • Mirin: 1 teaspoon
  • Dashi stock: ¼ cup
  • White sugar: 1 tablespoon
  • Vegetable oil: ½ teaspoon

- Soy sauce: ½ teaspoon

Directions:

In a bowl, thoroughly whisk eggs, sugar, mirin, soy sauce, and dashi stock. To dissolve the sugar, thoroughly whisk.

Heat a nonstick pan or omelet pan to a moderate temperature. Use vegetable oil to grease your pan, then add one layer of the egg mixture to the heated pan and spread it around the entire cooking pan.

Using a spatula, raise the egg layer up to almost an inch from the bottom (there should still be some liquid on top) and fold the end over the remaining egg layer. Push this omelet to the edge of the frying pan by rolling it until it ends. Repeatedly oil this pan and add another layer of egg. Allow it to solidify from underneath.

Miso

Cooking Time: 30 minutes
Servings: 4
Ingredients:

- One teaspoon of dried wakame
- Four cups of water and three tablespoons of miso paste
- Kombu: 1 (4 inches) of dry kelp
- 12 ounces of tofu (chunks)
- ¼ cup chopped green onions

Directions:

Heat four cups of water in one go over a low heat. Cook the kombu until the sauce begins to boil after adding them. After adding the bonito flakes to the kombu mixture, toss the well. After turning off the heat, leave this dashi for about five minutes. Pour through cheesecloth or a different type of strainer and set aside.

In a pot, preheat 3 ½ cups of dashi over medium heat. Tofu and wakame should be added and thoroughly combined. Take out one cup of the dashi, transfer it into a bowl, and stir in three teaspoons of the miso paste. Return this mixture to the daisy pot and thoroughly stir until they are heated. Add some green onions as a garnish and serve.

4

Chapter 3 – Japanese Sweet Stuff

Try these tasty and simple sweet Japanese recipes that are perfect for both novice and experienced cooks.

Salt Caramel

CHAPTER 3 – JAPANESE SWEET STUFF

This recipe is from the 47th chapter of Kitchen Palace and the 10th volume of Kitchen Princess Manga. Savor this unique combination of sweet and salty.

Cooking Time: 20 minutes
Servings: 8 to 12
Ingredients:

- ½ cup corn syrup,
- ½ cup unsweetened condensed milk,
- 2/3 cup sugar,
- 3 tablespoons butter,

- and 2 teaspoons salt

Directions:

Line an 8x8 baking pan with a baking sheet. Set it away. All of the ingredients should be cooked over medium heat in a saucepan. Turn down the heat to low and let this mixture sit for 20 minutes once the sugar has melted.

Stir the mixture carefully and regularly to reduce the liquid once it turns light brown. Turn off the heat as soon as the mixture becomes darker, then transfer one teaspoon of the mixture into a cup of cold water. Examine the mixture with your palm to see if it gets hard in water. The mixture is ready if it breaks easily. If the mixture is still soft, return it to the stove and reduce the heat. As soon as you.

CHAPTER 3 – JAPANESE SWEET STUFF

Black Sesame Pudding

Cooking Time: 1 hour
Servings: 4 to 6
Ingredients:

- Three tablespoons of water
- One teaspoon of gelatin powder
- ¾ cup milk and 2 teaspoons sugar

- Ground black sesame: 1 tablespoon

Directions:

Place the gelatin in a bowl and stir in three tablespoons water. Well combine them to form a paste. Set it away.

Transfer the milk, sugar, and sesame paste into a small pot and simmer it over medium heat. Add the gelatin paste to this mixture after thoroughly mixing to melt the sugar.

Stir this mixture constantly while cooking for an additional two minutes. Switch off the heat.

Place a pot of pudding in the center of a large pan that has been lined with ice.

To make this mixture thicken, keep mixing.

Transfer this blend into a single bowl and allow it to cool in the fridge for nearly forty minutes. To the serve is it applied.

Mugicha

CHAPTER 3 – JAPANESE SWEET STUFF

Cooking Time: 15 minutes
Servings: 2 liters

Ingredients:
- Two liters of water
- Mugicha: 1/3 cup of pearl barley or one tea bag

Directions:

Barley can be roasted on medium heat in a dry pan. Bake them slowly for almost ten minutes, until they are deeply browned. This roasted barley can be preserved in an airtight jar. You can add it to one jug of two-liter water to make cold tea. After filling the jug, let it sit for the night.

Put a Munich teabag in a teapot and add boiling water to make hot tea. Enjoy this tea after five minutes of absence.

Pockey

CHAPTER 3 – JAPANESE SWEET STUFF

Cooking Time: 1 hour 40 minutes
Servings: 30
Ingredients:

- 75 grams of plain flour
- and 2 tablespoons of sugar
- Slat: 1 pinch;
- 23 g of unsalted butter;

- 1 ½ teaspoons of milk

Directions:

Set one oven's temperature to nearly 350 degrees Fahrenheit.

Put all of the dry ingredients in a food processor and pulse them twice. In the machine, add the diced butter and pulse three times. Add milk to this mixture and pulse once more.

Place this homogeneous ingredients into a bowl and roll into a ball of dough. Place this ball of dough in the refrigerator for about half an hour.

Roll out the dough to a thickness of 5 mm, then trim off any excess to form a single rectangle. Cut 5 mm thin sticks, then put them out on a baking pan that has been buttered.

These sticks should be baked for around 20 minutes. Cover in chocolate that has melted and almonds.

CHAPTER 3 – JAPANESE SWEET STUFF

Dango

Cooking Time: 45 minutes
Servings: 6
Ingredients:

- 2 ½ teaspoons soy sauce
- ½ cup water; 1/3 cup sugar
- One spoonful of cornstarch or potatoes

- Six bamboo sticks

Directions:

In a bowl, combine rice flour and hot water. Allow the mixture to cool before kneading the dough with your hands. Work the dough until it becomes slightly firm, then form it into tiny balls. Bamboo sticks are an alternative if you are not able to form balls. After wetting these sticks, round them with dough balls.

Place these balls in a steamer and heat it to medium for nearly twenty-five minutes.

Delicious Mitarashi Sauce:

Fill a pot with ½ cup water and add soy sauce to it. Add cornstarch and sugar to this mixture now. Boil them to create a thick sauce. After adding the delectable Dango balls, serve.

5

Conclusion

Your kitchen will be more exciting and interesting when you prepare manga food. Rice, soy sauce, Sake, mirin, fish stock, Japanese mayonnaise, rice vinegar, ponzu, potato starch, and panko are among the materials you'll need for Japanese cooking. All of the equipment needed to prepare food, including pans, knives, cutting boards, and other items, should be in your possession. A wooden spoon, spatula, frying pan, kitchen utensils, and a few more equipment are required. Manga cooking is useful for making satisfying meals with a large number of ingredients and appliances. Try out the 25 recipes in this book to make delectable breakfast, lunch, and dinner dishes.

WRITTEN BY:
  Sophia Hudson

THANK YOU
THE END

www.ingramcontent.com/pod-product-compliance
Lightning Source LLC
LaVergne TN
LVHW020437080526
838202LV00055B/5242